What was it

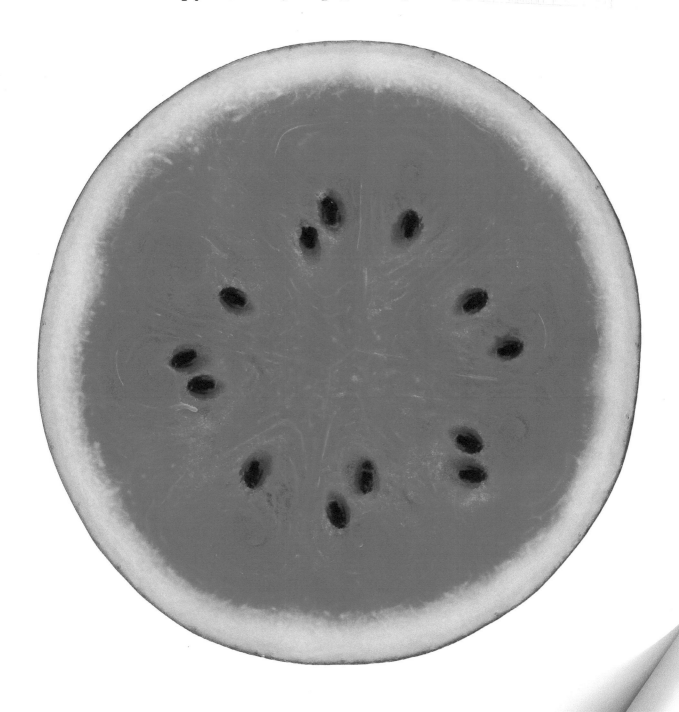

turn to see

What Was It Before It Was Cut?

by Kristen McCurry

PEBBLE
a capstone imprint

What do you think these things were
before they were cut?

Take a guess,
then turn each page to find out!

What was it?

 turn to see

A sheet of paper.

What can you cut out of paper?

What was it?

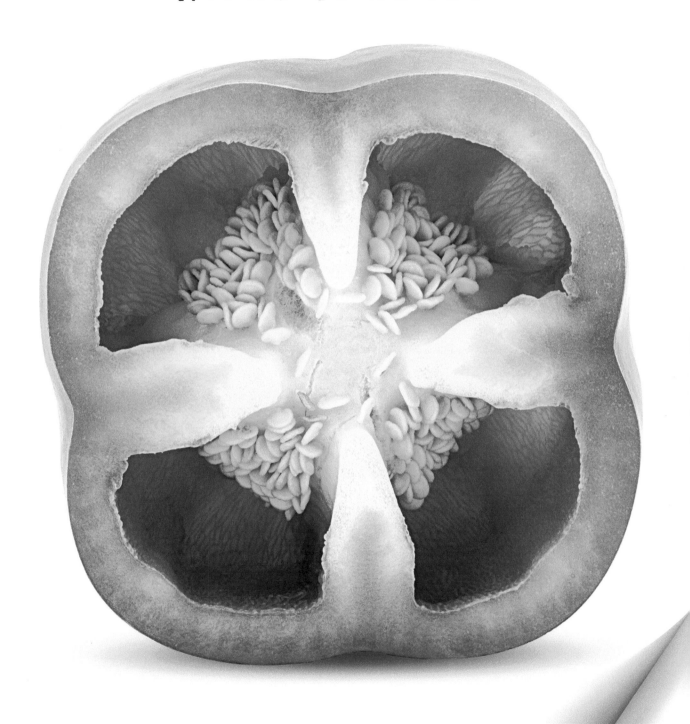

 turn
to see

What was it?

⇨ turn
to see

What was it?

⇨ turn to see

What was it?

⇨ turn
to see

What was it?

⇨ turn
to see

A rock called a geode.

Geodes have a surprise inside!

What was it?

turn
to see

What was it?

turn
to see

What was it?

 turn
to see

A block of marble.

Marble is a kind of stone.

What was it?

turn
to see

What was it?

 turn
to see

What was it?

turn
to see

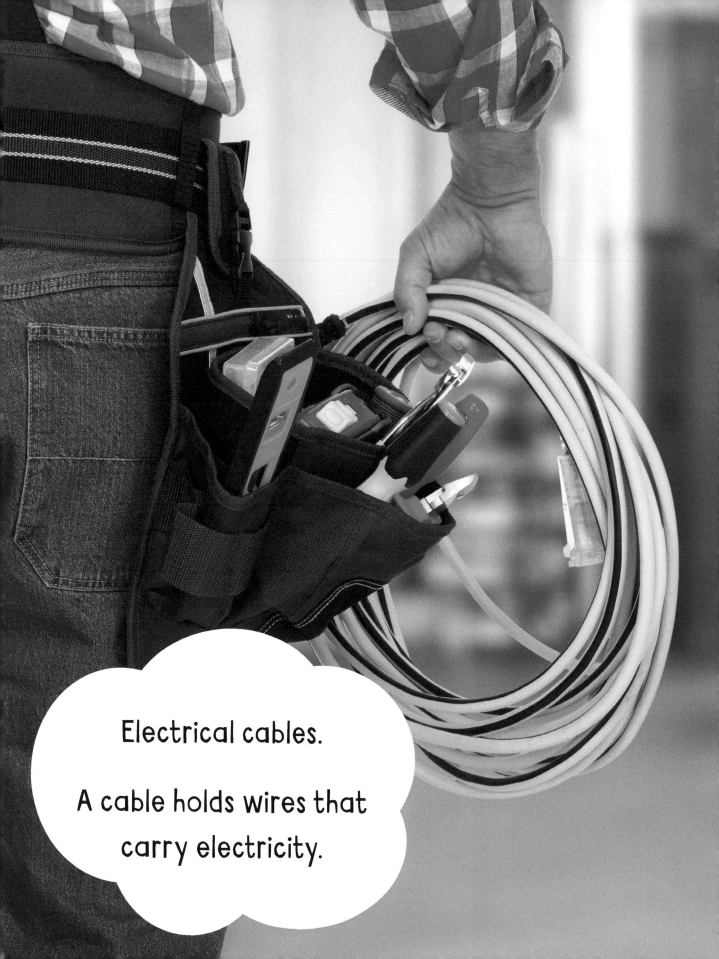

Electrical cables.

A cable holds wires that carry electricity.

What was it?

 turn to see

Good job! Try all the books in this series!

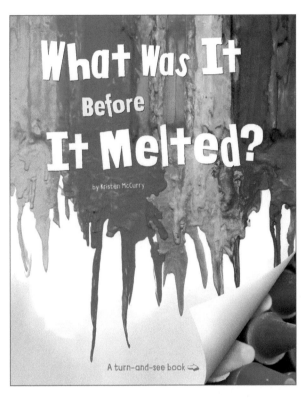

Pebble Sprout is published by Pebble, an imprint of Capstone.
1710 Roe Crest Drive
North Mankato, Minnesota 56003
www.capstonepub.com

Library of Congress Cataloging-in-Publication Data
Names: McCurry, Kristen, author.
Title: What was it before it was cut? / by Kristen McCurry.
Description: North Mankato, Minnesota : Pebble Sprout, a Capstone imprint, [2020] | Series: What was it? | Audience: Ages 4-8 | Audience: Grades K-1 | Summary: "Chop, slice, snip! Take a guess to determine what each object was before it got cut. These photo puzzles require mental dissection to solve!"-- Provided by publisher.
Identifiers: LCCN 2019044110 (print) | LCCN 2019044111 (ebook) | ISBN 9781977113313 (hardcover) | ISBN 9781977120137 (paperback) | ISBN 9781977113351 (pdf)
Subjects: LCSH: Shapes--Juvenile literature.
Classification: LCC QA445.5 .M427 2020 (print) | LCC QA445.5 (ebook) | DDC 516/.15--dc23
LC record available at https://lccn.loc.gov/2019044110
LC ebook record available at https://lccn.loc.gov/2019044111

Designer: Sarah Bennett
Media Researcher: Eric Gohl
Production Specialist: Tori Abraham

Image credits
iStockphoto: Dafinchi, 15, Wavebreakmedia, 20; Science Source: Ted Kinsman, 9; Shutterstock: Africa Studio, cover (bottom right), Alberto Stocco, 19, Alex Konon, 21, Aphichart, 25, barbajones, 22, Bildagentur Zoonar GmbH, 30, Brent Hofacker, 18, Brocreative, 10, Kozlik, 14, kurhan, 28, MakroBetz, 17, MaraZe, 29, Matka Wariatka, 6, Mita Stock Images, 5, Olga Guchek, 7, Olivier Le Queinec, 11, Photo Smile, 26, Schlegelfotos, 24, Standret, 12, Superheang168, 3, Tanya May, 16, Tim UR, cover, 13, Tomo Jesenicnik, 1, Toongna Online, 4, Triff, 23, vldkont, 27, YanaG, 8,

Design Elements: Shutterstock